HARD BREAD

PHOENIX **POETS**

A SERIES EDITED BY TOM SLEIGH

HARD BREAD

PEG BOYERS

THE UNIVERSITY OF CHICAGO PRESS

Chicago and London

PEG BOYERS is executive editor of *Salmagundi*.

The University of Chicago Press, Chicago 60637
The University of Chicago Press, Ltd., London
© 2002 by The University of Chicago
All rights reserved. Published 2002
Printed in the United States of America

11 10 09 08 07 06 05 04 03 02   1 2 3 4 5

ISBN: 0-226-06964-8 (cloth)
ISBN: 0-226-06965-6 (paper)

Library of Congress Cataloging-in-Publication Data

Boyers, Peggy, 1952–
        Hard bread / Peg Boyers.
            p.   cm.—(Phoenix poets)
        ISBN 0-226-06964-8 (acid-free paper) —
        ISBN 0-226-06965-6 (pbk. : acid-free paper)
        1. Ginzburg, Natalia—Poetry. 2. Women authors—Poetry.
        3. Authors—Poetry.
      I. Title. II. Series

    PS3602.O94 Y68   2002
    811'.54—dc21

                                                            2001037606

For Robert

and for our children

Contents

IV

Acknowledgments

Grateful acknowledgment is made to the editors of the following magazines in which these poems, sometimes in slightly different form, first appeared:

The Boston Phoenix Literary Supplement: "Reading Elizabeth Bishop" and
  "Elegy"
Leviathan Quarterly: "Coat"
Michigan Quarterly Review: "He Hates, He Loves"
The New Criterion: "The First Thing to Go"
New England Review: "Last Words"
The New Republic: "Apparition: View from San Miniato"
Notre Dame Review: "The Dream of Music"
Ontario Review: "Adult Children"
The Paris Review: "Open Letter to Alberto Moravia"
Partisan Review: "Letter to a Suicide"
Sewanee Review: "Memoria: Regina Coeli Prison"
The Southern Review: "Journal Entry: London, 1960," "Letter to a Damaged
  Daughter," "Offertory: Blood Oranges," and "Letter from Amherst,
  1976"
Western Humanities Review: "Caro Leone" and "Translation"

* * *

My debt to the friends who helped me throughout this project is too enormous to express with dignity. You know who you are: please accept my deepest thanks.

All but the last of these poems are spoken by the Italian writer Natalia Ginzburg (1916–1991). Much is based on Ginzburg's life and writings; much is invented. (Detailed information about the sources and circumstances of these poems, including translations of Italian phrases, appears at the back of the volume.)

Ginzburg's first husband was killed by fascists in 1944; her second died in 1969.

I

Coat

At eleven I learned to lie.
Disobedience and its partner,
deception, became my constant companions.

How enormous then that first transgression,
against Father's command, a sin damning as Adam's:
walking to school alone.

We *all* lied, mother explained,
it was . . . *necessario*.
How else to survive

Father's rages,
his sweeping interdicts
and condemning opinions?

Oh sweet allegiance of lies:
siblings and mother bound
together in a cozy tie!

My brothers' lies
were manly,
obdurate, built to last.

Mother's were infirm little things,
infected from birth by her obstinate grace,
fated to die as soon as they hit the air.

But this lie, the lie about *me*, was sturdy,
knit, as it was, from the fiber of maternal love
and a wife's defiance.

Go ahead; it's right.
Walk alone. Grow up.
Each assurance a coercion, each coercion a shame.

The lie was a coat of mail
I'd don each day, threading my arms
through its leaden sleeves,

pulling its weight over my head,
steeling myself
for my father's wrath.

In it I was strong and getting stronger,
but tired, always tired.
Oh to rest, shuck the lie and confess!

Father forgive me, I knew not what I did!
At night I'd rehearse the lines
and pray for his cleansing fury.

In the morning I'd meet him in the hall,
already crabby in his gray lab coat,
barking his harsh observations

about my robe (pink: ridiculous)
about my face (vacant)
about my voice (inaudible).

Mother, how did we produce such an insect!

I was used to this.

Exasperated, he would stuff his red frizz into a beret,
hurl himself into his loden cape
and bolt out the gate—too rushed for truths.

Silenced again, I would resume my solitary mission,
lugging my books, wearing my lie to school
and back again, through the maze of city streets.

One day the mist briefly lifted and I saw
the winter sun pulsing silver and pale
through a hole in the sky—a quiet disk

hopeful as the moon.
A face emerged, white whiskers smiling,
familiar, professorial—an angel perhaps,

or a friend of the family—
here to guide me safely
across the river to school.

He took my bag and my arm,
allaying my fears with talk
calculated to soothe, flatter, amuse.

Gentile, cosí gentile.
Ever faithful, he met me at my gate
morning after sweet morning.

We chatted carelessly the whole way,
intimate as lovers,
never a snag

or worry to hold us up—
I, grateful and happy,
he gently leading the way.

My trust deepened daily with his purpose
and burrowed
in the snug darkness of short days

where the new lie took root.
From deep in the loam, the probing
stem pushed to the surface.

Meanwhile, the first lie grew light with practice.
And my coat assumed
the comfort of a uniform.

His purpose, obscured from the start by fear,
suppressed tenaciously
by innocence—canny innocence—

flared up in a question,
betraying an ignorance
both clear and obscene:

"Little Girl, would you touch me — here?"

Suddenly my hand, sweetly warming
in his flannel pocket, was pushed
to the hard, oozing center.

My hand recoiled.
But the ooze stuck.
In that minute my childhood ended.

I ran home as fast as my legs would carry me
to hide my shame in the place
where secrets were made and kept,

willful little liar, disobedient
sinner trying to find my way alone
through fog, through lies.

My life was filling up with secrets
and deceit's secretions,
loneliness and melancholy.

I hugged my coat tight against my body
so that the lies and I were one.

Offertory: Blood Oranges

In the courtyard the March
trees are heavy with fruit.
The blossoms and their scent have
gone the way of this brief winter,
escaped past loggia and clerestory.
What remains is solid, disconcertingly
material. Let the painters have these ornaments,
turn their formal features into art.

I want something else.

Ecco le sanguinelle! Sono mature, Signora.
Give me the blood oranges, the soft
pocked ones at the grocer's,
ripe with hope, their russet blush
barely hiding the blemishes.

Mature fruit, maturing fruit,
lend me your gentle optimism.
Let your acrid breath blow
cynicism out of reach, burn despair.
Let your juice quench the soul's
thirst for bitterness.

I lose my way in my own neighborhood.
A map to me is a forbidding web of coded lines
for sleuths and cognoscenti to unravel.

If I dare ask anyone directions
he loses his temper
and says I have no patience for puzzles.

Before going to a foreign city
he studies guide books and prepares lists
of all the essential monuments.

He plots intricate walks
past the houses of dead composers,
artists and writers.

He brings bouquets to the graves of heroes.
Then I photograph him: posed, loyal,
before the tombs of his beloved deceased.

Sometimes I catch him
conducting great symphonies
from the couch in our living room.

He waves his pencil furiously at the imaginary
percussion section, shouting, "Forte!"
From the strings he beckons a tender crescendo.

I understand nothing of music,
painting is a mystery and theater
often bores me to the point of asphyxiation.

For me there is only poetry,
though all I can remember
are random fragments.

He recites all of Shakespeare
in flawless English, complete
with simultaneous Italian translation.

I retain only two things: the alphabet
and an aria from *Lohengrin* my mother used to sing me
which I perform on request, out of tune, and with fervor.

He loves change, adventure, and travel.
I love sameness, routine, staying at home.
Nevertheless I follow him around the globe

dragging myself to museums (where I quickly find the book shop)
and lectures (where I covertly write stories while "taking notes")
and concerts (where I fall asleep) to please him.

After each performance at the opera he runs
backstage to congratulate the singers
who seem, all of them, to be his friends.

I watch as he stands there
laughing and joking with people
dressed as cardinals and soldiers and kings.

He knows me completely,
knows that I am lazy, undisciplined
and infinitely distractable.

My Psychoanalysis

For a long time I resisted psychoanalysis.
The vanity of stoicism
kept me away.

Therapy embarrassed me—
its confident promise of cure
a blithe insult to my permanent condition.

Something repellant in that cozy premise—
as if talk could erase sorrow,
a purchased intimacy annul pain.

Eventually I succumbed.
Neurosis was
not without its appeal.

Sadness,
by comparison, was—
well, sad.

For months I rambled on
about my childhood losses
—the house on Via Pastrengo, its garden,

the idleness of pre-school days,
father's cleansing rages,
mother's healing songs.

Outside the office window, Saint Peter's
beamed its message of forgive and forget.
Bernini's maternal colonnade reached out

to gather me in its safe embrace,
tempting me to the eternal womb.
The single obelisk struck

its Catholic shadow across the piazza,
a ready compass
to direct my confession.

Inside, the good doctor traced
my symptoms to traumas, instructed
me in the ways of cathexis and hysteria,

walked me down Oedipal Lane, pausing
at the corner of Penis Envy and Desire
—irrelevant intersection

for a widow
dead now to Eros and its foils,
wed instead to absence, to abstinence.

We turned down other paths,
past Delusion and Regret,
Melancholia and General Disorders.

I began to recognize the territory.
At last I located an inadequacy
suitable for treatment.

My problem was profound.
Its source, the blanket.
Blankets, I confessed, were my nemesis.

The skill of folding had eluded me.
Order was not my domain.
Was it not insane?

With apologies to Dr. Freud
we embarked on my practical cure,
matching corner to woolly corner,

holding the satin border tight, pressing
down hard to make the crease,
not releasing until the job was done.

Over and over we opened the closet,
shook out the blankets, stretched
them out between us, then slowly,

slowly folded them back together.
Stepping forward, stepping back,
a sarabande to master a modest task,

a stately dance to put away the past,
each fold another trouble to press,
order, and repress.

Dottore, La ringrazio la sua cura!
I never thanked you properly.
Who thanks the analyst?

Now your goateed face smiles
benignly from the morning obituary.
It says you were from Friuli.

I hear your guttural accent
—teacherly, Jewish—
almost Viennese.

II

He Hates, He Loves

for Pier Paolo Pasolini

My friend loves the fragrance of refuse,
the stench of public urinals and the musk
of skunk the way I love violets and hyacinths.
He hates all that is feminine, delicate, soft—
except when disguised as a rough embrace.

My friend loves the poor, really *loves*
them: He eats with thieves and sleeps
with whores. He says they are "natural",
understand what is holy
and good in life.

My friend hates limits, deferential lies,
the daily imposture, tact.
He believes in creative, restorative indecency:
the anesthesia of anonymous sex,
the oblivion of a Bedouin's tent.

My friend loves the bridges of Rome—
their sooty marble, baroque with seamy underworld friezes—
where he can lose himself in the verdigris
surface of the Tiber, the dull
shimmer of cupolas in its dirty scum.

He hates the north,
dim cities, paltry light,
heavy industry, stalled desire.
He craves sharp insinuations,
the wanton curl on a boy's brow.

My friend loves the south, the humid nights
and hot urban days. Whatever is
fetid or fermenting he favors. The friction
of pants boiling in the sun, consumed by shade,
the wet chests of workers heaving by the docks.

        He inhales their sweat like incense, breathes-in
        the sacral purity of their scent.

My friend fears his lover's wife, hates
pretending he loves her to keep his lover near.
When they meet he kisses her powdered cheeks.
This is his compromise, his cross.

My friend loves to stroll along the embankment
in Trastevere, pausing at the parapet to
sniff the nape of an insolent neck, the sulfur
stink of hair glazed with too much brilliantine.

He loves to gaze at the virile bulge of crotch,
buttocks and muscle, the sheen of worn denim.
He hates the charade of romance, indulges
the perverse chastity of refused attachment.

He hates and loves, loves and hates,
hates the loving, loves the hating.
He loves what I hate. I hate his loves.
He loves men. I love him.

The Theater of Words

The theater of words
is retrograde.
Dead.
That's what you said
after we'd gone to see
Goldoni at the Pergola.

You spoke of *gesture*,
risk,
the sacral,
theater of cruelty.
Terms that made me yawn
before I understood—

What rite were you performing
that day in Sicily
when they beat you to a pulp,
left you at the roadside,
a smear of carrion
for jackals and crows?

Journal Entry, London (1960)

This country wears on me.
Everywhere system, clockwork.
Reliable grind of wheel on wheel:
clerks count pence, cordial and precise,
passersby deliver accurate directions.
No life in the exchange,
no dance between cheater and gull,
the game of rogues
only a memory shared by vacationers
in Italy. Where honesty's a habit
there's no sport in lying.

Yesterday I saw her, La Grande Signorina.
She stood at the grocer's,
filling her cart with produce,
meat, cereal, beer.
I wanted to say to her, "Miss Burnett,
your novels, they are, *come si dice*, *così*
inglesi. Your sinister families delight, their bad manners
and sordid motives speak to me. Their rude
talk harsh and true. Dialogue a relentless hammer
nailing them to their destiny like a cross.
Colloquial atrocities snapped like snake bites.
Without compromise. Good.
Made in England. *Qualitá*."

But I did not say these things.
I was mute. I let her pass, a bustle
of wool, slightly rank with body odor.
The scent of industry, I thought, not a lazy
smell. She was working even there, plotting
domestic horrors while she shopped.
Let her work then. Why
distract her with my foreign patter?

Be polite. Avoid encounter.
Shrink from analysis.
Respect privacy. Hide misery.
These are the lessons decreed
by drizzle and fog.
Follow the Thames,
become dull.

That he personified bourgeois aestheticism
was a cruel commonplace among Marxist literati.
This was both true and untrue.

He himself was so securely bourgeois
he lived comfortably as a bohemian,
relinquishing with ease the material comforts.

Thus he hardly noticed when his fortune dried up,
and took to poverty as if it were merely
a new convention, a necessary imposition

to be endured, without resentment.
In this sense he was passively
ascetic; his virtue was routine.

Society—its ceremonies, its conscience—bored him.
Nothing nauseated him more
than the words *Avanti Popolo!*

As a narcissist, however, he was a failure.
When he peered into the mirror
for reassurance, his reflection dissolved mercilessly

into peals of helpless laughter.
The absurd was never far from his line of vision.
Laughter was his glory and his refuge.

In the end, when his gaze met the abyss
with frankly desperate certainty, I like to think
the abyss welcomed him, smiling its ironic smile.

Ode to Ernest

Too bad I wasn't a man.
A man might have won your favor.
But I was (I am) just a woman.
Not even your kind of woman.
And, in the end, you were not
my kind of man.

That summer in Venice
I'd have come duck shooting with you
in the marshes on the edge of the lagoon,
crossed the Piave
to the low country—across the river and into the trees—
if invited.
I'd have flown off to Spain,
sat in the sombra with you at the bullfight,
endured the irritating banderilleros
and the idiot torero with his bloody bull's ears.

But you were after bigger game
and games.
Always the chase, and then
the let-down aftermath of triumph.
And then again the chase.

Maybe I was too brainy
or too ugly, or
just too much an editor for you to notice
my adulation.
That time at Harry's in '48
when we met over proofs and revisions,
you lobbied for a Guernica cover,
pressed again your terms for payment.
I wanted to tell you how you made me,
made my prose, cleaned it till it was lean.
I composed my English sentences,
rehearsed the grammar and pronunciation.

> *Mister Hemingway, you are to me a giant.*
> *I learn what is the world from your books.*
> *I learn what is to see from your books.*
> *Your words, they are clear, filled with light*
> *—like Venezia!—*
> *and limpid, too, as water.*

But you went on (and on) about details and then
about the old days
—the Great War—
canals jammed with bodies,
Venetians and Austrians,
face down and right side up,
floating colossi, bloated and dead.
The waste of it.

All those stories about the waste of it.

Years later, in Paris:
another novel, another meeting.
The paperwork and then the talk.
The bar-wise exuberance
and pennywise nit picking repelled me.
You were having a bad day with your bad eye,
the one you injured boxing at seventeen,
the one that failed
the army physical,
the one tuned-in to failure.

I can still feel the weak eye
wandering off course
while the strong eye held its bluff.
It was the weak eye that drew me
with its furtive doubt
—while the strong eye kept aloof,
focussed on the action, got on with it,

that lonely, predatory eye,
always looking (and loathing),
stalking the world, nailing it with words,
punching it out fast and clear,
staccato (like you, Ernesto)
disconnected, *mai*
legato.

Letter to a Suicide

for Cesare Pavese

Cesare, how uncomfortably you wore
your name, its ill-fitting opulence
a perpetual scratch on your skin,
its imperial resonance a daily burden.
Roman grandeur irritated you. Better the soot
and toil of Turin, sweeter its meager allure.

Yours was another aristocracy,
the one that luxuriates in despair and disdains
the coarse economy of effort and reward.
How we bored you with our easy banter
and banal satisfactions. Our fraught intimacies
seemed exuberant to you, saccharine our enthusiasms.

Prince of denial, you mistook the negative
for the noble, reveling in the perverse elitism
of *nulla*. What is it to renounce life
when you have never truly lived? Cesare,
this death you purchased is cheap. Another
instance of your incorrigible parsimony.

Once again you've escaped without
settling your accounts. And we're stuck
with the bill. Well, not exactly. You paid
plenty—if pain can be called your currency.
Generosity was never your strong suit.
Avarice another way of holding back on life.

Even your handshake was stingy: a mere
two fingers proffered reluctantly, then quickly
withdrawn. Never a full, lingering hand's worth.
Something furtive in that gesture, as if you were
sneaking friendship against the rules,
like the covert reach for tobacco, the nervous,

hurried tamping of your pipe. Uncomfortable
pleasure, futile nicotine to tear the veil of *ennui*.
Imperious One, Heavy Wit, your last joke
was no fun. This august death, oh Caesar, the final pun.
You sent us off on *ferie*, confident that the *Strega* prize
had distracted you from death. But the winning

made you stronger. Useless now the refined style of
restraint, the flat dry cool of prose. Suddenly literal,
the longed-for gun come home at last to greet your temple.
Irony finally resolved. Ellipses closed. Oh Caesar. *Cesare*.
August life, august death. Selfish *stronzo*.
Cretinous egotist. Pathetic, cherished ass.

For Primo Levi

> And till my ghastly tale is told
> This heart within me burns.
>
> —Coleridge

Cool now,
old heart;
your tale is told.

That uncertain hour—predicted, awaited,
arrived—over, and over again,
is passed now, through.

Away, agony.
Burn no more.
Rest, memory; escape

the chasing incubus, the replay of striped
deaths, indelible hand stain on shirt front.
A rag, you said. *To use a man as a rag*—

Lungs, discharge
the eternal stench of smells
down there.

Hush, voice. No need to endure
the weary rasp of throat
worn out, repulsed

by the language that fed it, that starved it—
toten Sprache, schöne Sprache—
ears, enjoy your repose.

Fade now.
Leave the Technicolor
remembrance to others.

Let go,
relentless eyes, let the torturing
pigment drain at last. Release

even the pale monochrome images
before and after the Lager—
the ones you hugged so tenaciously

so as to banish
the garish camp print,
vanquish the vividness of *then*.

Forsake strength. You're allowed
to be finished.
We can survive *for* you.

Let us answer the guilt accountants,
the ones who'll
weigh your motives

as if experience could be measured
with a ledger,
pain assessed on a scale.

Be generous.
Allow us this assistance.
Coraggio. Go ahead.

Dissolve, old self.
Now answer your new vocation:
become *our* memory.

The Voice in the Arbor

for Elsa Morante (1918–1985)

Early autumn in Piazza Navona:
Neptune's fountain still pumping
freshwater oceans
indifferent to the chill.

I edge away from the splash,
pull my chair closer to the café door.

The damp is closing in on the memory of summer.
Last month you sat here,
under the arbor
      —it was just another dry Roman night—
ordering your spinach *molto bollenti,*
your imperious smile genially insistent
as always, and then
straight to the issue:
my play.

Let me tell you the truth,
You have no gift
for drama. Non é il tuo pane.
Your characters are static; they do nothing
but talk incessantly like walking novels.
Go back to fiction!

I hated you in those moments
and loved you.

Your furies always
healed me, their hard words
scouring the system.
Hurt a state from which I could emerge
whole again.

The trace of your voice hangs shrill in the arbor.
The mist from Neptune's trident hits my face, cold and true.

Open Letter to Alberto Moravia

La Stampa, July 14, 1971

Dear Alberto,

It's true: I am a coward. The other night,
at dinner, I neglected to tell you how much
I detest your latest novel. Had you asked me,
I would have found a way to say something not
exactly false, but less than true: *You've done it again!*
A tour de force! But your thoughts were already
elsewhere, in Persia perhaps, or Turkey, where
your translators would soon greet you, whirling
at the airport, with garlands and rare oils, adoring dervishes
ready to anoint you their new Byzantine king.

Great One, Monolith
                    —*ormai amico dopo tanti anni*—
you still frighten me. Impatient mentor, enormous
nourisher: your power paralyses. I owe you
my honesty, but I shrink from the physical you.
Forgive me this public confession.

Now that you are away in Arabia with an Arab,
I'll tell you what I think, here, in the newspaper.
They say a public place is always best
for the most intimate fights. Yesterday
I overheard a pair of estranged lovers at the corner
rosticceria as they hammered out the terms of their separation
while the waiter served them antipasto, polenta, ossobucco.
The civility of eating taming the occasion.

Aglio e origano, basilico

e pomodoro, would that you could flavor my words.

Alberto, you have lost your way—you, our *dopoguerra* beacon.
Publicity, that siren, has seduced you.
You have not only written a bad book;
you have betrayed your vocation.
You say the book's a comedy. It is not.
I hear no laughter here, only the inexorable grind of contrivance.

This book is a lie. It has no truths or truth.

False muse, get thee gone;
free the famous from his fame.

You will say that you worked five years to produce
this work, that I should grant you that. To which I answer:
Five years writing are five years of pleasure.
Your reward is in the doing.

I am not *unduly harsh.*

Understand me: this is a love letter.
My criticism, my embrace.
You are the Original, I the copy.

You are evaporating, Alberto. Stop before you disappear!

You were always the most limpid, genuine, of men.
Now this persona studs
your soul like so many rhinestones.

Adorned one, adored one.

This crassness in you confuses.
This magazine self, the one
in the interviews, devours the serious core.

Conformista, Indifferente.

Come back.

This is my slap. Cry now to show me you breathe.

Natalia Ginzburg
Rome

Reading Elizabeth Bishop

You have no intellectual curiosity.

That's what she said.
My friend, the thinker. She's right.

I take my hurt to poetry,
but the verdict is confirmed.
Guilty as charged.

It's true: I hate the new.

Bishop chases the unfamiliar like a Cheshire her canary—
compelled to know the song and eat it too.

Imagine studying the tropical hummingbird,
razorbill auks and mailed armadillos;
looking at nature and everywhere finding metaphor.

I see a waterfall and it remains a waterfall.

A wall is a wall in Rome or Rio.
Man made it, time will tear it down.

The first geography is the neighborhood,
the provincial, my province.
Dream of home and stay at home.

Explore the familiar, discover the strange.

How does one marriage dissolve
while another renews itself?

How can a banker and a painter emerge
from the same union?
Is this boring?

Then it's boredom I love,

the underside of the uneventful,
the inside of zero. Emptiness,
let's face it, is underrated.

This American teases with her elegiac conditional:
What might have happened had she not traveled,
what she would have missed.

Nostalgia's pathetic enough over real past.
Why miss experience twice removed?

Miss, instead, the life you missed
by removing yourself, willing change,
willing interest with dogged persistence.

And what of meaning?

Did you really think, poor orphan,
that the world was a classroom,
and history your teacher?

Did you never learn,
years after that time at the fishhouse
when the sea seduced you
with its epiphanous language and narrative ruse,

that knowledge is a rock,
never flowing, never flown?

Letter from Amherst, 1976

Formal expanses surround the churches here.
Insipid lawns, desolate and vast,
hum with voracious mosquitoes. No crowded piazzas.
No towers tangling the horizon. No markets.
One lone steeple points, accusing heaven.
No stones, no stucco—only stark, mortal
wood, vulnerable yet forbidding.

In this town, it's the negative that's real.
Absence
fills out the shape of things.
Emily Dickinson's stolid words
haunt the landscape, her ghost scratches
the starched dress displayed in the museum,
disdaining frills, modest as her pen.

I always hated her frugal verses,
replete with wrens and annoying honeybees,
fastidiously parsing their divinity
across the dainty page, their holy industry
comical, repellent. Rhyme a vice
to contain ardor. Meter a stingy
trick to lock-in feeling.

I fell for the subterfuge, mistook economy
for parsimony, spurned what was pared down,
chiseled to fit her tiny breast. I doubted
a despair so tame it answered to her call,
sorrow transparent as gossamer, harsh
and quiet as wind. I mistrusted a wit so
nimble it could thread a spire, and not be pricked.

Now, in this place, I hear the steady
measure of her line. Feel its weight.
Iambs march diligently after meaning, beat out
the boundaries of hopeless desire, pain's
inexorable rhythm. The poet's work her salvation.
Busy lady, lovely insect.
Poor ironic fly caught in amber.

Amherst's translucent fossil.
Grief's brittle imprint.

III

Caro Leone

Pizzoli, Gli Abruzzi. November 20, 1943

Today the post arrived with a card
from Mother. From you, nothing. Last night
I slept with a vague sense of your being
near. A dreamed voice said something tender,
I recognized the timbre, not the words—
for tenderness was never in your repertoire;
that Russian rasp did not lend itself
to lovers' gush. Where did it come from

then, this new register of emotion, this
dream from another place, where harshness
is leveled soft, compromised? Why do you
not write? Have you an address for me,
or are you where place and distance have no place?
Is time nothing to you now? Excuse
the impatience. In spite of my fears,
I write. A trick to postpone grief? Perhaps.

I will not feel bereft. Not yet.
Usually I manage to convey some note of cheer
or news—a tale about the children, a joke
heard from the *postino*, anything to make

the tone seem unrehearsed. Forgive me
these lines, tired by now from the strain
of frivolities designed to stifle
curses I can't allow myself to spit.

How can I will off the weight
on my temper of this Abruzzi winter,
confinement to this safe province while you,
my love, confront the devil in Rome?
I want you here, in this stupid home
where the measure of my desire is
desolation, the shutters beating out
the vespers to the last chapped stutter.

All my love, Natasha

Prison Box: Inventory

Rome, February 1944

copy *War and Peace*,
cyrillic type
(fading, spine bent)

cashmere scarf,
arm length
(dirty, white, torn)

photographs of a girl,
two boys
and a woman (frayed at the edges)

pencil stubs
(carbon
tips spent)

lined spiral notebook
(nine pages left,
yellowed, blank)

pair of wire-rimmed glasses
(left lens shattered,
nose support gone)

pack of Nazionales
(empty,
crushed)

matches
(full box,
intact)

comb (teeth mangled)
shaving blade
(no cup, no brush, no mirror)

cordovan shoes
(soles shot,
laces missing)

undershirt
(sleeveless, ribbed,
pungent still—)

black beret
(shapeless now,
oiled with the scent of his hair)

shetland
turtleneck
(gray, twisted)

beige pants
(knees worn, wool
soaked in his blood)

Memoria: Regina Coeli Prison

On such a day, an ordinary day,
men come and go in the city streets;
they buy food and newspapers; they rush
to their appointments, faces flushed, pink lips full.

On such a day you dressed
in custodian uniform,
entered the prison, went to his cell.
You saw the hard bed where he had lain

and the blank wall he watched day
after day, and the barred window
beyond eye level through which his hope leaked
month after month.

You lifted the sheet to look at his face,
leaned over to kiss him in the usual way.
But it was the last kiss.
It was the usual face, just a little more tired.

And his clothes were the ones he always wore,
and the shoes were the ones he always wore,
and the hands were the ones
that broke the bread and poured the wine.

Today, still, during the hours that slowly pass,
you lift the sheet again,
and then again:
you look at his face

for the last time
and feel again the cold last kiss,
the press of stiff mute lips,
and then again the sheet.

If you walk down the street,
no one walks next to you;
if you're afraid
no one takes your hand.

And the street is not yours;
and the city is not yours:
not yours the city of lights;
the city of lights belongs to others,

to the men who come and go
and buy food and newspapers.
You can look for a while out the quiet window,
look in silence at the garden in the dark.

Before, when you cried, there was his voice.
When you laughed, his diffident smile.
But the gate that opened each evening will stay closed now forever.
And your youth has become a deserted house—fire out, shutters sealed.

Translation

Rome, December, 1945

It was after our wedding I began
translating Proust. Each day I'd unfold
pages of the great *foglio protocollo,*
fill them with Italian equivalents.
The foolscap watermark, my emblem.
Each night, your corrections—honest,
harsh—set me back, pressed me forward.
The sixteen volumes a challenge
disguised as a present from a friend
with better French than mine. My first
assignment. The romance of red leather,
the scent of literature. Gilt framing
my fancy ambitions. I never mastered
this craft: what I was after was the thing
itself, never the thing transformed.

When you were sent to the Abruzzi,
I followed with the Ghiotti dictionary,
two books from the Gallimard edition
and the children. If only I could do
this much, I thought, some day I might
complete the job. But life—and death—

had still to do their work on me. While you
were in Rome, relentless, subversive,
I pored over Swann and Odette, the idiocy
of passion. Instead I might have dwelt
on you, on our superior union, on the way
your wiry hair would scratch my neck
when you bent to kiss my breast. Even on
the ironic scoffs you'd lavish every time
I came to you begging for approval.

Now the war is over; my translation begins
anew. How to bend this world into words?
Where is the language for loss, longing, futile
desire? The seasons' metaphors run dry;
what remains is bare text, stark with nouns
and too few verbs. Work will set you free.
Arbeit—
A neighbor saved the manuscript.
The Germans overlooked the flour sack. Now
I'll turn to what I began. For you. At least
those first two books. What to call *Geneviève*?
Can a *madeleine* ever become a *maddalenina*?
Here on the Via Uffici del Vicario what more
is there to do? The children are in Turin.
We'll make Proust Italian. What else can I change?

Anniversary: March 24, 1984

For the 335 Italian civilians shot by the Nazis on March 23
and March 24, 1944 at the Ardeatine catacombs outside of Rome.

Roll back the stone.
Witness the drying remains.
Scratch the names of the lambs on the sarcophagus wall:

Michele Di Veroli and his father, the tailor,
Professore Gesmundo and Aldo Finzi,
the Di Consiglio from Trastevere, a family of street peddlers,

the spies, the communists, the Jews
—always the Jews—
plus two more for good measure

rounded up near Saint Peter's:
for the *todescandidaten*
in prison were too few. Too few.

Oh absent, careless Lord,
I consign these names to your care.
Miserere nobis.
And damn the murderers once and for all.
Is it only the fool who sayeth in his heart

there is no god?
You eat up our people like bread.
God thou art ungodly.
                              Dona nobis—

No peace for the dead
buried without ritual.
Blasphemy, how meager your comfort.

At least grant them a limbo
of like-minded sinners.
And spare them the company of saints. Amen.

Black Shirt

Black shirt. Opaque,
forbidden uniform.
Smooth as a boot.
Gun cold, dead serious.
Yoke and sleeves
cut sharp to fit a *duce's* fancy.
Martial fashion styled to flatter.

Black shirt, black shorts.
Black ticket, black price.
Coveted suit, *squadrista* erasure
in the spin of common longing,
glamorous Empire dreams
puffed by a sawdust Caesar.
          Oh secret, fascist youth!

I yearned to belong to the order,
sing the songs, play the patriot,
twirl in a circle of birch rods.
Pretty fasces, little janus ax
gleaming its double blade,
strutting a sycophant's salute
to the beat of a lictor's drum.

Instead, I wore protest white,
absent color right for a cipher
forced outside the whirl
by a father's merciless principles.
Tyrannical resistance
—too righteous to feel right,
mistaken as punishment.

Inside the white, I willed
my own subversion,
flapped my jumping jacks
with desperate purpose,
made myself a white flag
fluttering a stupid surrender:
      Take me. I'm tired of the tireless denial!

Poor mortified rebel,
scurrilous girl, innocent still
of the smut and pitch of war,
unworthy brat resistant only
to your family's refusal.
Easy collusion blankly sought,
reluctantly relinquished.

Black shirt, black lie.
Don today the suit of mourning.
Wear it well. Know now
the color you so long desired.
Cancelled pigment, cancelled life.
Use the widow's veil in vain to
hide the scug and shame of memory.

IV

Elegy

Little made thing, tissue without
sinew or bone. Genetic trace.
Helix of features. Matrix of inherited
vectors, blob of original plasma, desire's
excreta, quiet now, still.
Born without pulse. Toothless,
lungless, breathless one.

But there was blood there,
and perhaps a soul—and it was mine.

Wasted, unwanted one. Blank
page. Holy, chaste, unmade thing.
I am undone by the memory
that is not you.

The sins against oneself cannot be forgiven.

Live now in the spaces, hated creation,
loved progeny. Limn the interstices.
Inhabit the physical borders.
Stupid fruit, unripe, unfinished,
unconsecrated, formless thing.
The vessel was refused you.
Your home is limbo. Now go.

Letter to a Damaged Daughter

My womb was worn out
by the time it housed you.
Two wars, two husbands,
too much, too little, too late.

I might have tricked time,
pushed you through
before the scythe struck your brain,
missed the crucial chromosome.

But the cell went unsplit.
Non-disjunction. Freak mitosis.
Punished
refusal to divide.

We blew and blew
our thoughts into you,
a team of holy ghosts
praying to inspire.

Oh for a flame to fan! But the light
was out. Only darkness where a mind
should be. What resides there?
What's inside a head gone dead?

What makes you smile, little idiot?
Wherefore your optimism, your joy?
I'd wished hard for a girl,
pictured curls in lacey ribbons, romps through

frills, smart glint in eye to match mine,
quick wit to cut the maternal ties
when the body was ready.
But the snipped cord still binds

me like a noose—I want to loosen it,
cry out for you to undo the knot,
but you look on, stone dumb,
laugh, and give it another tug.

What bargain did I lose?
Perhaps I mis-spoke, and God took you
for some other purpose. Iphigenia,
the war is still raging, the sea is not calm

and the winds do not favor travel.
The joke's on me, little sacrifice.
Forgive me. I mis-made you, sweet
miscreant. Endure, now, my sad devotion.

Apparition: View from San Miniato

From the hills on the left
poplars keep watch over the city.
The Arno drags its mud to the horizon;
crew teams labor in the June sun.

We read the short histories of children
written on gravestones,
take in their pictures still vivid under glass,
imagine their survivors—gone
as the garlands once laid here.

Where are the parents who erected
statues for the betrothed
thwarted by war, facing each other
in futile supplication,
apart for the first time and forever?

In the distance a tornado of sparrows
whirls over a garden
somewhere near the green-white
glimmer of a bell tower,
dissolves and regroups, pours

into the cloister, splashes out again,
the funnel overflow rising back, dispersing
into flutter and glide, and then back
to the black vortex
for the precipitous dive to the panic center.

Adult Children

The moment they were born
age struck us
like an incurable disease.
Along with age, terror.

Never before had we felt terror like this:
Terror at our age,
terror at our immense, fragile
power.

When we were apart from our children
we felt suddenly
less old
and not at all powerful.

But the terror persisted
rumbling underneath—
a river of magma,
dark and inexorable.

We longed to crawl into our parents' laps
and tell them of our terror,
but we were too large for their laps
and besides, they were dead.

Our children, whose
grown-up laps are
longed-for but off-limits,
are appalled by our neediness.

It dawns on us that of all people
in the entire world
only they, whom we love most,
are wholly unable to give us comfort.

This thought
strikes us as the heaviest,
most exhausting thought
possible.

It weighs on us
like the oldest star in the universe
and tires us, but in the end
makes us feel grounded and powerful again

as oaks—
and ancient,
and secondary,
and gray.

Our own hunger, thirst
and exhaustion which our parents regarded
as primary are banished to a zone
where none may cast a glance.

We have become—even to ourselves—
simple, colorless
nonentities,
bound to the dominion of time.

The Dream of Music

Never ask my name.
—*Lohengrin*

I sleep at the opera.
The problem is the music.
I just don't get it.
I am a person who should *love* music.
I'm sensitive enough—and smart.
You could say I'm an artist.
I was *meant* to love music.
Perhaps it's *music* that doesn't love *me*.

Did I inadvertently rebuff it
the one time it paid me a visit?
Maybe, through some tragic mistake,
music was on its way to me and got sidetracked,
distracted into landing on some other spirit.
Perhaps, by some lapse
I missed its presence
and it slipped away unnoticed.

Once, on a tour of the Forum,
I ducked into a temple to say a prayer to Orpheus.
I asked him to descend on me with his lyre,

thrill me with his song.
I was a siren on the ruins, waiting to be ravished.
But my prayer went unanswered.
Later, I learned it was mis-addressed.
My fate, musically speaking, was sealed.

Jealous Apollo, god of music,
accept my corrected prayer!

It's not that I don't try.
I do.
Year after year, I renew
for the season
because I love *being* at the opera.
By now the opera house itself is dear to me,
our box the host of countless
stolen naps and covert dreams,
red velvet seats perfect for opulent reverie.

Sometimes, I approach the opera with genuine determination.
I concentrate hard on the voices,
the interplay of plot and histrionics.
For a fleeting moment, I imagine
my struggle is paying off, that music's
seduction is but a note away.
I *almost* hear what others hear.
I know that I am about to achieve tremendous pleasure.
This pleasure will be as immense and fathomless as the sea.

Next thing I know,
I'm drowning in sleep.

In my dream I am Elsa with her Wagnerian knight,
his breastplate resplendent with theatrical reflections,
helmet protruding virile horns.
He sings me the conditions of our union.
I trill my ecstatic compliance.
I am at home in mystery.
I don't care who he is or what to call him.

Last Words

The god whom we should love is absent.

—Simone Weil

Dear Ones,
Please indulge me one last time.
I am ashamed to tell you
that in the end I have capitulated.
Yes, given in. Resorted to baptism—
again, and for the first time
for grace rather than convention.

The faith of my mother, stoically
resisted all these years, has overtaken me.

It's true, I am a Jew.
Whenever anything happens
to the Jews I feel directly
that something terrible has befallen
my people. And yet, at this moment,
I understand that mine
has been an essentially Christian life,
concerned with essentially Christian goals.

To say these things is to betray something
real in me: I am a Jew. My father was a Jew.
My husband, your father, was a Jew.
We have suffered unspeakably and borne witness
to horrors. We are confirmed by history.
We do not forgive.
                    And yet, we must
forgive.
I'm too weak to resist the soul's desire to absolve,
to be resolved.
My children, forgive me this forgiveness.
To forgive is to relinquish a certain integrity.
I hereby relinquish it.

It's not that I'm afraid of the afterlife,
or that I necessarily believe in The Afterlife.

Nor have I come to this through some silly wager
leaping to faith
when the rungs on Pascal's ladder
ran out, each logical line
another step towards heaven.

I've suffered no conversion.
Rather, I have accepted what was always there,
what I was too ashamed to admit.
I am, God help me, a believer.
Belief has sustained me through life's reversals.
Whatever strength I have had
belief has been its source.

I'm not strong enough to be a real Jew.
My Jewishness arises from pathos,

longing for what is irrevocably lost,
loving Vishniac's shop keepers,
the boy with his hands up,
the world I never had—
the guilt in not having lost *that*.

Now let the waters wash away
the sins of regret,
the hypocrisy of denial.
Baptism, be my confessor.

Epilogue: L'Intervista

(interviewing Natalia Ginzburg)

You smoke.
You smoke and then cough.
You smoke and you cough and

we talk. We talk and you
smoke   —*your cigarette, your ash*—
   and you cough.

We're in one of your plays,
a star-struck girl and her idol.
I hasten to cover my adulation,

put on my best Italian. Oh ancient
tongue of civility! Oh refuge
of vowels and wet rhythms!

In this language my dull questions
brighten, their original pallor
invisible now under centuries of manners,

the brio and texture of genteel exchange.
Italian, with its liquid impetus,
is a ready medium for improvisation,

and you jump in on cue, swim in the fluid
encounter, buoying me up in a surround
of comfort food and questions

about my childhood, about my child.
The thin inquiry gives way
to conversation. We talk. We eat.

The *tortellini* slide down easily
and the veal is fragrant with rosemary.
Primo Levi and Pavese

arrive with the *contorno*.
Pasolini provides the sweet,
Visconti, *il vino*.

Elsa Morante and Moravia
take their places at the table,
and gnomic Calvino, too.

Your cousin, Montale,
hovers in the corner,
grinning the critic's grin—

Florentine flaneur, in for some mischief
with the fictionists. The din
escalates, memory's contentious noise.

You smoke and you cough.
Outside the church bells begin their
celestial counterpoint.

Rest beckons.   *Come back soon.*
Bring your son
   —when I am well again.

But you do not get well. Your ash, Natalia.

NOTES

Although Natalia Ginzburg was born in Palermo in 1916, her childhood was spent in the northern industrial city of Turin where her father was a medical researcher. Ginzburg wrote more than once about her 'chaotic' upbringing in a household which was 'nothing'—neither Catholic nor Jewish, neither rich nor poor. Her family was actively anti-fascist (her father and one of her brothers served prison time) and fiercely non-sectarian.

In her early twenties, she married Leone Ginzburg, a Russian scholar, intellectual and political activist and with him had three children. Through him she entered the circle of friends which, in 1937, founded the Einaudi publishing house, where she worked as an editor almost all her life. During the war Leone was repeatedly interrogated, eventually put under house arrest, and finally captured, tortured and killed by the Nazis months before the Allied victory.

After the war Ginzburg wrote many novels, plays, essays, and newspaper columns on a great variety of subjects. She also occasionally translated from French and was instrumental, with her colleagues Cesare Pavese and Giulio Einaudi, in bringing many American authors to the attention of Italian readers. In 1950 she married a Shakespearean scholar named Gabriele Baldini with whom she had two children. Baldini died of hepatitis in 1969. In 1987 she was persuaded to serve as a representative in the Italian parliament where she was known for her outspoken and iconoclastic views, often in defense of the poor and disenfranchised. Her voice in Italian is plain and direct, astringent yet passionate. Though she was inclined to discursiveness, she was easily distracted into metaphor and anecdote.

This is not a biography and the particulars in the poems are for the most part invented.

p. 6, "Coat"
Gentile, così gentile: Kind, so very kind (with the added understanding of "nice" or even "refined").
p. 8, "Offertory: Blood Oranges"
Ecco le sanguinelle! Sono mature, Signora: Here are the blood oranges. They are ripe, madam.
p. 10, "Essay On Marriage"
This poem begins as a verse transposition of "Lui e Io" ("He and I"), Ginzburg's often anthologized prose portrait of her marriage to Gabriele Baldini, but then follows its own course.

p. 17, "My Psychoanalysis"

Loosely based on an essay by Ginzburg of the same title.

Dottore, La ringrazio la sua cura!: Doctor, I thank you for your cure!

Friuli is a northern province of Italy formerly part of the Austro-Hungarian Empire.

p. 27, "Journal Entry, London (1960)"

When Ginzburg lived in London for a year she developed a taste for the novels of Ivy Compton Burnett, about whom she wrote an essay entitled "La Grande Signorina."

come si dice, cosí inglesi: how do you say it?—so English

Qualità: (high) quality

p. 29, "Let Us Mourn An Unknown Writer"

When Delfini died, Ginzburg reread his work and wrote an essay for the newspaper, *La Stampa,* in which she openly regretted having underappreciated him in life.

Avanti Popolo (literally "Onward People") was a slogan for the Italian risorgimento, the Italian independence movement; it was later appropriated by the Communist party.

p. 32, "Ode to Ernest"

Ginzburg was Hemingway's editor at Giulio Einaudi Editori.

The Piave is a river in the Veneto region.

Harry's Bar, a legendary gathering place for Americans and other tourists and émigrés in Venice, was frequented by Hemingway in the '40s.

staccato: separate

mai legato: 'never connected'; in music, notes played *legato* are played as if joined to one another.

p. 35, "Letter to a Suicide"

Ginzburg and Pavese worked together as editors.

ferie: vacation days, often a full month, taken by Italians in August.

The *Strega* prize is perhaps the major literary prize in Italy. Ginzburg herself won it for her autobiographical novel, *Lessico Famigliare* (published in English as *The Things We Used To Say*). Although this poem has it that Pavese shot himself, in fact he committed suicide by taking an overdose of sleeping pills.

stronzo: turd

p. 37, "For Primo Levi"

toten Sprache, schöne Sprache: death language, beautiful language

p. 40, "The Voice in the Arbor"

The novelist Elsa Morante and her husband, novelist Alberto Moravia, were among Ginzburg's closest friends.

molto bollenti: boiling hot

non é il tuo pane: it's not your thing (literally, *not your bread*)

p. 42, "Open Letter to Alberto Moravia"

La Stampa: newspaper published in Rome for which N.G. wrote a regular column

ormai amico dopo tanti anni: by now a friend, after so many years

aglio e origano, basilico e pomodoro: garlic and oregano, basil and tomato

dopoguerra: postwar

Conformista, Indifferente: Conformist. Indifferent (or apathetic).

(*Il Corformista* and *Gli Indifferenti* are the titles of two of Moravia's best known novels.)

p. 53, "Caro Leone"

For Leone Ginzburg, see opening note.

Pizzoli, Gli Abruzzi: A small village in a remote province where Leone Ginzburg was sent and put under house arrest as a result of his anti-fascist activities. Natalia and the three children accompanied him there, but when Mussolini fell and the Germans occupied Italy, Leone resumed his subversive political work in earnest, printing and distributing a clandestine newspaper in Rome.

postino: postman

p. 58, "Memoria: Regina Coeli Prison"

This poem is closely modelled on "Memoria," one of the few poems Ginzburg wrote. She wore a disguise and sneaked into prison in order to see her dead husband one last time.

p. 60, "Translation"

Ginzburg began to translate *A la recherche du temps perdu* shortly after she was married. She completed the first two volumes and then abandoned the project. (Her translation is still available in Italy.)

foglio protocollo: foolscap paper

Arbeit: German for work. The words "Arbeit macht frei" (Work makes you free) appeared over the gates of Auschwitz and other Nazi camps.

p. 62, "Anniversary: March 24, 1984"

todescandidaten: the prisoners who were potential candidates for execution by the Germans

p. 64, "Black Shirt"

duce: Mussolini's preferred title

squadrista: fascist youth group

fasces: A bundle of birch or elm rods containing a double ax carried by the lictors or attendants of the Roman Emperor. The fasces was used as an insignia of authority in ancient Rome and adopted by Mussolini as the emblem of Italian fascism.

p. 69, "The First Thing to Go"

brutta: ugly

p. 71, "Elegy"

Ginzburg's first child with Baldini died in his first year. This poem laments a child lost, or aborted, in utero; whether Ginzburg had such an experience I do not know.

p. 72, "Letter to a Damaged Daughter"

This poem is addressed to Ginzburg's daughter, Susanna, who was born brain damaged. The biological particulars refer to downs syndrome, which may or may not correspond to Susanna's condition. Susanna was the second of two children fathered by Baldini. She continued to live with her mother until her mother's death in 1991.

p. 74, "Apparition: View from San Miniato"

The church of San Miniato overlooks Florence from a hill south of the Arno. The cemetery there is distinguished by its funerary sculpture and the elegance of its family mausoleums and tombs.

p. 76, "Adult Children"

This poem is both a distillation and an embellishment of Ginzburg's essay of the same title.

p. 79, "The Dream of Music"

Never ask my name: In the opera *Lohengrin*, the hero warns his beloved Elsa not to ask his name lest the spell that will end their happiness come into effect. But Elsa's curiosity gets the better of her and brings on the opera's tragic conclusion.

Orpheus: According to Greek and Roman myth, Orpheus was given the first musical instrument, a lyre, fashioned by Hermes. He was reputedly such a great singer that he out-performed the sirens. But Apollo, not Orpheus, was the god of music.

p. 82, "Last Words"

Ginzburg's mother was Catholic and her father Jewish, but she was brought up in a strongly non-sectarian household. Although she converted to Catholicism in order to marry her second husband in the Church, this poem (and also the earlier poem, "Essay on Marriage") imagines that the conversion did not 'take', that she had tried to remain a Jew until almost the end of her life. *Vishniac's shop keepers, / the boy with his hands up:* now vanished Eastern European Jews documented in the photographs of Roman Vishniac.

p. 85, "Epilogue: L'Intervista"

contorno: side-dish, usually a vegetable